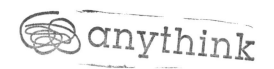

TURNING POINTS IN U.S. HISTORY
GREAT DEPRESSION

by Veronica B. Wilkins

pogo

Ideas for Parents and Teachers

Pogo Books let children practice reading informational text while introducing them to nonfiction features such as headings, labels, sidebars, maps, and diagrams, as well as a table of contents, glossary, and index.

Carefully leveled text with a strong photo match offers early fluent readers the support they need to succeed.

Before Reading

- "Walk" through the book and point out the various nonfiction features. Ask the student what purpose each feature serves.
- Look at the glossary together. Read and discuss the words.

Read the Book

- Have the child read the book independently.
- Invite him or her to list questions that arise from reading.

After Reading

- Discuss the child's questions. Talk about how he or she might find answers to those questions.
- Prompt the child to think more. Ask: What did you know about the Great Depression before reading this book? What more would you like to know?

Pogo Books are published by Jump!
5357 Penn Avenue South
Minneapolis, MN 55419
www.jumplibrary.com

Library of Congress Cataloging-in-Publication Data

Names: Wilkins, Veronica B., 1994- author.
Title: Great Depression / Veronica B. Wilkins.
Description: Minneapolis, MN : Jump!, Inc., [2020]
Series: Turning Points in U.S. History | Includes index.
Audience: Ages 7-10.
Identifiers: LCCN 2019020738 (print)
LCCN 2019022363 (ebook)
ISBN 9781645271406 (ebook)
ISBN 9781645271383 (hardcover : alk. paper)
ISBN 9781645271390 (pbk.)
Subjects: LCSH: Depressions–1929
United States–Juvenile literature.
United States–History–1919-1933–Juvenile literature.
United States–History–1933-1945–Juvenile literature.
Classification: LCC HB3717 1929 .W46 2020 (print)
LCC HB3717 1929 (ebook) | DDC 330.973/0916–dc23
LC record available at https://lccn.loc.gov/2019020738

Editor: Susanne Bushman
Designer: Jenna Casura

Photo Credits: Everett Historical/Shutterstock, cover, 16-17 (foreground); Alan Fisher/New York World-Telegram and the Sun Newspaper Photograph Collection /Library of Congress, 1, 11; FPG/Hulton Archive/Getty, 3; ClassicStock/Alamy, 4; Chicago History Museum/Getty, 5; DEA PICTURE LIBRARY/Getty, 6-7; Photo12/Universal Images Group/Getty, 8-9; Harris & Ewing/Library of Congress, 10; Everett Collection/Age Fotostock, 12-13; Minnesota Historical Society, 14-15; Valentin Agapov/Shutterstock, 16-17 (background); farakos/iStock, 18; R. Gates/Hulton Archive/Getty, 19; robertharding/Alamy, 20-21; Minneapolis Star Journal/Minnesota Historical Society, 23.

Printed in the United States of America at Corporate Graphics in North Mankato, Minnesota.

TABLE OF CONTENTS

CHAPTER 1

END OF THE ROARING TWENTIES

In the 1920s, many Americans lived comfortably. They enjoyed entertainment. Young people spent evenings dancing to jazz music.

People had enough money to buy expensive items, like cars. They **invested** money in the **stock market**. We call this time the Roaring Twenties.

The Roaring Twenties came to a crash in October 1929. The New York Stock Exchange floor was chaotic. Everyone was shouting. Why? Stock prices were falling. People wanted to sell their **shares**. They wanted their money out of the stock market. They were afraid of losing it.

Too many people sold at once. Too few bought. Shares became worthless. The stock market crashed. People lost a lot of money.

New York
Stock Exchange

soup kitchen line

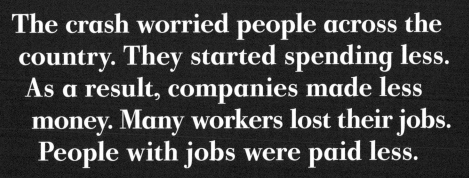

The crash worried people across the country. They started spending less. As a result, companies made less money. Many workers lost their jobs. People with jobs were paid less.

The country entered what is known as the Great **Depression**. Many did not have enough to eat. Long lines formed at **soup kitchens**.

DID YOU KNOW?

People rushed to banks. They wanted their money out in cash. These were called **bank runs**. Banks did not have enough cash. Many closed. This hurt the **economy**.

CHAPTER 2

A POOR NATION

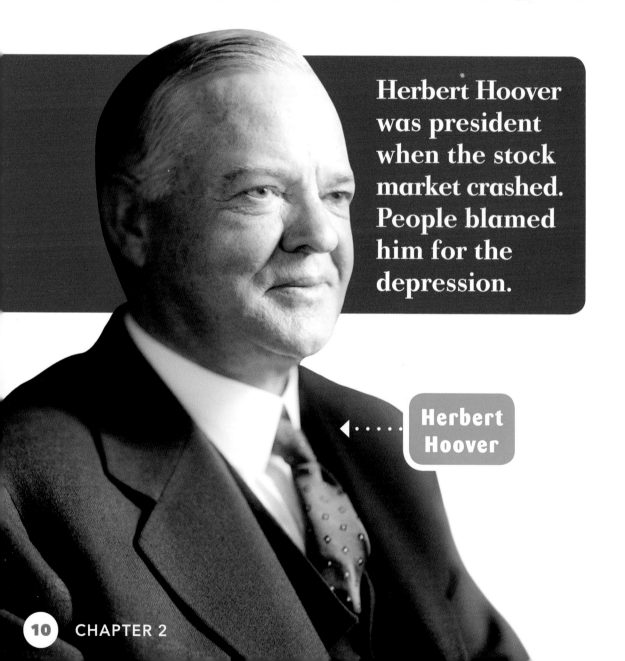

Herbert Hoover was president when the stock market crashed. People blamed him for the depression.

Herbert Hoover

People found ways to save money. But many still lost their homes. Some illegally rode trains across the country. Why? They were looking for work.

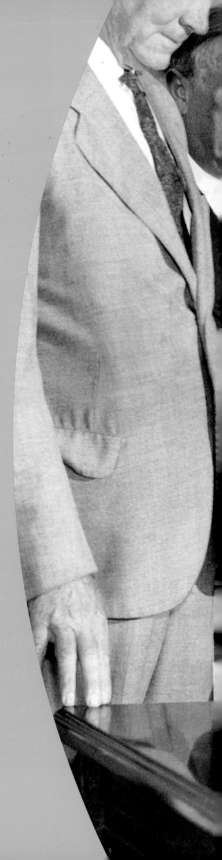

Franklin D. Roosevelt became president in 1933. He had a plan to help people. He called it the New Deal. First, he closed banks for a few days. This stopped the bank runs.

The New Deal created new programs. One gave money to help the poor. Another bought extra food from farms. This supported farmers and helped those in need.

WHAT DO YOU THINK?

Roosevelt spoke about the New Deal on the radio. He called the American people his friends. How do you think people responded to this?

Franklin D. Roosevelt

Some programs gave people government jobs. The Works Progress Administration (WPA) was one of these. WPA workers built new bridges, roads, and sidewalks. New schools improved communities. Public art made cities and towns more beautiful.

Roosevelt also created social security. He signed the Social Security Act into law in 1935. This set up a new system. Money came out of workers' paychecks. They got it back when they **retired**. Posters told Americans about it. Social security is still important today!

WHAT DO YOU THINK?

The U.S. government created the minimum wage in 1938. This is the lowest amount companies can pay workers. We still have this today. Do you think this is a good idea? Why or why not?

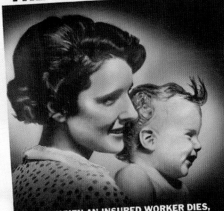

CHAPTER 3

NEW DEAL PROGRAMS HELP

No one event ended the Great Depression. New Deal programs created jobs. Roosevelt stopped basing the **value** of money on gold. These acts helped rebuild the economy.

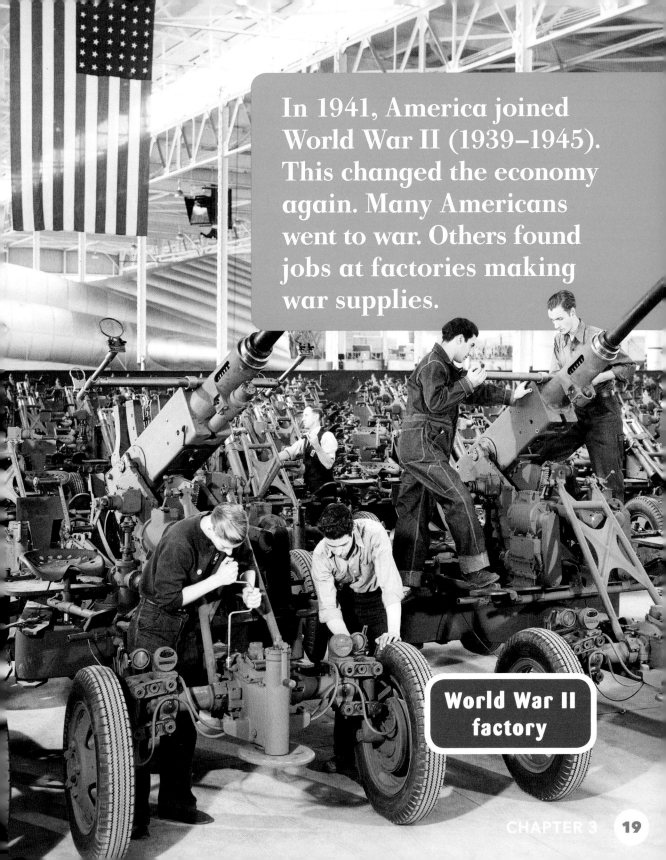

In 1941, America joined World War II (1939–1945). This changed the economy again. Many Americans went to war. Others found jobs at factories making war supplies.

World War II factory

The Great Depression lasted 10 years. It changed America forever. How? The government now helps more people. We still visit places made by New Deal programs. The San Antonio River Walk in Texas is one! How or where do you see the effects of the Great Depression?

San Antonio River Walk

TAKE A LOOK!

Look at **unemployment** rates during the Great Depression. How did the New Deal and World War II affect these rates?

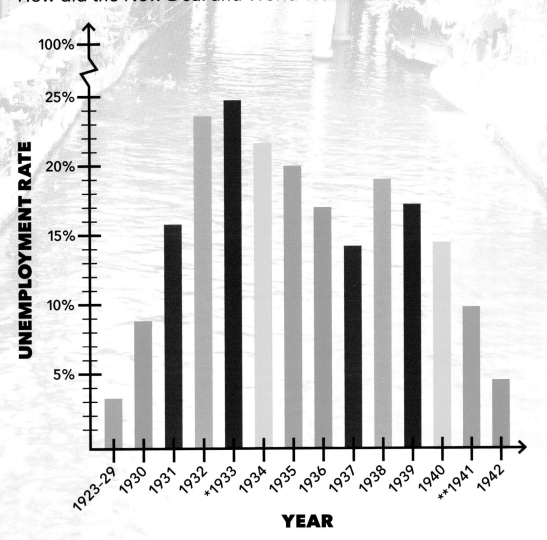

*1933: The New Deal begins. **1941: The United States enters WWII.

QUICK FACTS & TOOLS

OCTOBER 1929
The stock market crashes. Many people lose their investments. The United States enters the Great Depression.

MAY 6, 1935
President Roosevelt establishes the Works Progress Administration to build new infrastructure, such as roads, bridges, and airports.

JUNE 14, 1938
The Fair Labor Standard Act sets a national minimum wage for the first time.

1933
One in four Americans are unemployed.

SEPTEMBER 1939
World War II begins in Europe.

MARCH 4, 1933
President Franklin D. Roosevelt takes office. Two days later, he closes banks to stabilize the economy.

DECEMBER 7, 1941
Japan bombs Pearl Harbor, Hawaii. The United States responds by joining World War II. Factories begin making war supplies, creating jobs and helping rebuild the U.S. economy.

AUGUST 14, 1935
President Roosevelt signs the Social Security Act into law.

bank runs: Times when many depositors try to withdraw their money from banks because they fear that the banks will fail.

depression: A time when a country's economy shrinks and many people lose their jobs.

economy: The system of buying, selling, making objects, and managing money in a place like a country or state.

invested: Gave or lent money to something, such as a company, with the intention of getting more money back later.

retired: To have stopped working, usually because one has reached a certain age.

shares: Some of the many equal parts into which ownership is divided.

soup kitchens: Places where free food is served to the needy.

stock market: The system of buying and selling stocks and shares in companies.

unemployment: The state of being unemployed, or without a job or paid work of any kind.

value: The worth of something.

INDEX

TO LEARN MORE

Finding more information is as easy as 1, 2, 3.

1 Go to www.factsurfer.com

2 Enter "GreatDepression" into the search box.

3 Choose your book to see a list of websites.

FACT SURFER